A Place Called Knowing:
Discovering Your Identity In Christ

By
Jane Weeks

With
Illustrations By
Molly Chamberlain

A Place Called Knowing: Discovering Your Identity In Christ
by Jane Weeks

Printed in the United States of America

ISBN 1-594679-94-0

All Scripture references are adaptations taken from the inherent meaning of the cited verses (or portions of the cited verses), unless a verse is quoted in its unedited entirety, in which case the translation is noted after the reference.

Taken from Prayer Portions, © by Sylvia Gunter, The Father's Business, P.O. Box 380333, Birmingham, AL 35238, E-mail FathersBiz@cs.com, or www.thefathersbusiness.com

www.xulonpress.com

Michelle,
Eph 3:18&19

For Mama
You brought me to Jesus. There is no greater gift.

Acknowledgments

Beverly Fettig
Thank you for your prayers, insight, and wisdom.
Thank you for showing courage in the face of my *effervescence*.
You tell me like it is.

Maria Cremers
You did the hard work and left the flowers to me.

Dale and Judy
It is a rare and precious thing to be among those
who listen for His voice, and follow Him.
Luke 6:23

Gary Flohr
Your kind spirit is captured in every picture you take.

And

Carrie
For speaking words of life;
I praise Him for your extraordinary love.

Foreword

People today are in a rush. They are seeking quick answers to difficult problems. If the "fix" isn't instantly apparent, they run to some other possible source. Some have a vague idea that there might be answers for them in religion, in God. But religion has left them empty and adds to the non-relenting pressure to perform. God seems unreachable, and the Bible is too often a closed book.

Where does one find God in a hurry?

In a condensed format that can be easily accessed, this book contains powerful scripture that will provide the life changes we all crave. Each entry can be read in just a minute or two. The message of Christ's love will restore the weary. The truly hungry will find food in these pages that will give them strength to pause. The earnest seekers will be drawn in and will find Him who is life – and the truth that will set them free.

The heart of this book is God's love toward us. My prayer is that its message will be heard above din, and quiet the soul of the reader.

-Beverly Fettig -

Introduction

God knew His children were in need of deliverance. He knew that we had forgotten who we are. God knew satan had come and stolen the identity of His children. And so He whispered to a servant: *"Tell them."* Not just this one servant, but many of His beloved have heard His voice resound with the same cry:

"Tell them.
Tell my people who they are.
Tell them they are mine.
They have been bought and paid for by the blood of my Son.
Tell them that I love them and that I want a relationship with them.
Tell them to talk to me. I will hear them and I will answer.
If they look for me with their whole heart,
they will find me.
I am close by and I will never leave them.
Tell them that I knew all about them,
even before I formed the earth.
They were my idea from the beginning.
I created them for eternity, to be close to me.
Tell them they are my children and I long to hear from them.
Tell them that I will come for them one day soon.
And I will take them home with me where they belong.
We will live together for eternity and there will be
no more sorrow."

When a servant hears the heart-cry of his beloved Master, he can only respond in loving obedience. Once you have felt His breath on your face, nothing and no one can deter you from the quest He has set before you.

In those battles fought in high places, we learn to put on *His* armor. We can bring nothing to the fight except a willing heart. But, it is within the heart that God's spirit dwells and is brought to life. *No weapon formed against us can prosper.* And so here it is: this little book. May its words find a home in your spirit and settle into your deepest ***knowing.***

*I pray that you may grasp how wide and long
and high and deep is the love of Christ.
Ephesians 3:18, 19 NIV*

As you take this journey, come boldly to the
Throne Of Grace and say…..

Because Of Christ I Am…..

A

Accepted ...

Wherefore *accept* ye one another,
as Christ also ***accepted*** us
to the glory of God.
Romans 15:7 KJV

How often we stand in judgment of others.
*Christ **accepts** me with all my faults and failings.*
I am commanded by God to accept everyone in the same way.
How do I do this?
It is a constant remembering where I could have been,
if not for grace. I, in turn extend that same magnificent
grace to others. I can look at them as my equal
in the divine favor of God's mercy and grace.

A

Because of Christ I am...

Able to do all things ...... Philippians 4:13

Abounding in grace ...... II Corinthians 9:8

Abounding in hope ...... Romans 15:4, 13

Abraham's offspring ...... Galatians 3:29

Acknowledging my need for God ...... Matthew 5: 3, 6

Adequate ...... II Corinthians 3:5

Adopted ...... Galatians 4:5

Adversary of the devil ...... I Peter 5:8

Alien and stranger in the world ...... I Peter 2:11

Alive in Christ ...... II Corinthians 5:20

Always having sufficiency in all things ...... II Corinthian 9:8

Ambassador for Christ ...... II Corinthians 5:20

Anointed ...... I John 2:27

Anxious for nothing ...... Philippians 4:6

Assured of reward ...... I Corinthians 15:58

Assured of success in Him ...... Proverbs 16:3

B

Bought With a price ......

For ye are **bought with a price**:
Therefore glorify God in your body,
and your spirit, which are God's.
I Corinthians 6:20 KJV

God created me. I belong to Him.
He gave me this precious life.
But I sold myself as a slave to sin.
I left Him!
I wandered around and did hideous things
with the life He had given me.
It was my body that should have been broken.
I am the one who sinned.
He did nothing wrong.
Yet, He came to **buy me** *back!*
He suffered. He poured out His blood.
He was broken for me.
I am no longer my own, because
I was **bought with a price.**
I am branded by His love and I wear His name.
My very life and breath should be a
picture of His glory.

B

Because of Christ I am …

Baptized into Christ …… Romans 6:3

Beautiful …… Eccl. 3:11

Becoming a mature person …… Ephesians 4:13

Becoming conformed to Christ …… Romans 8:29

Blameless at His coming …… I Thessalonians 5:23

Blessed …… Jeremiah 17:7

Bold and confident …… Ephesians 3:12, Hebrews 4:16

Bond servant ……Psalms 116:16

Born of God …… I John 5:19, John 1:12, I John 4:7

Born Again …… I Peter 1:23

Branch, part of the true vine …… John 15:5

Bride of Christ …… Isaiah 54:5, 62:5b

Brother of Christ …… Hebrews 2:11

Built up …… I Peter 2:5

C

Clean ......

You are already **clean** because of
the words I have spoken to you.
John 15:3 NCV

*I cannot go back over the past 20 years
and un-do the terrible things that I have done.
I cannot take back the harsh words or anger.
I cannot un-divorce.
I cannot un-hurt all the people I have hurt.
I cannot fix any sin that I have committed.
God knows this, so do you know what He did?
He sent a Savior to die for me!
Because I have accepted Jesus,
and I have repented of my sins,
God has forgiven my past!
Nothing remains of the old me.
I am **clean**!*

C

Because of Christ I am ...

Called ...... Romans 1:6, I Corinthians 1:9

Cared for with compassion ...... I Peter 5:7

Carried ...... Exodus 19:4

Cherished ...... Ephesians 5:29

Child of God ...... John 1:12

Citizen of Heaven ...... Philippians 3:20

Clay in the Potter's hand ...... Jeremiah 18:6

Cleansed ...... John 1:7, 9

Clothed with Christ ...... Galatians 3:27

Comforted ...... II Corinthians 1:4,5 & Matthew 5:4

Confident ...... Proverbs 3:26

Conformed to His image ...... Romans 8:29

Continually with God ...... Psalms 73:23

Controlled by the love of Christ ...... II Corinthians 5:14

Created in Christ for good works ...... Ephesians 2:10

Crucified with Him ...... Galatians 2:20

D

Drawn by God ...

No man can come to me,
except the Father which hath sent me ***draw him***;
And I will raise him up at the last day.
John 6:44 KJV

Here is another thought that goes straight to my heart.
*God **draws** me to Himself.*
He calls my name. He yearns for me, and so
He does marvelous things to entice me to want Him in return.
*The Greek word for **draw** in this scripture is*
*"**helko**" meaning "**To take for oneself**"*
God looked down and singled me out.
He pointed to me with His mighty hand and said to His son,
"I want this one."

D

Because of Christ I am ......

Dead to sin – Alive to God ...... Romans 6:6, 11

Delighted in ...... Isaiah 42:1

Delivered ......II Timothy 4:18

Desired ...... Psalms 45:11

Dead, and my life is hidden in God ...... Colossians 3:3

Disciple of Christ ...... Luke 9:23

Disciplined in love ...... Hebrews 12:5,11

Drawing near with confidence ...... Hebrews 4:16

E

Empowered to obey ...

... because God is working in you
to ***help you want to do***,
and ***be able to do***, what pleases Him.
Philippians 2:13 NCV

*The constant temptations that
bombard us and interrupt our
lives are inevitable.
God knew we could not overcome
temptations on our own.
Look what He has done!*

He *works inside of us to create
a desire to do good.*
He *works inside us to
give us* ***His*** *power to
fulfill those desires that are pleasing to Him.*
He does the work!
He gives the power!

E

Because of Christ I am ...

Enlightened ...... Ephesians 1:18

Enriched by Him ...... I Corinthians 1:5

Encouraged ...... II Thessalonians 2:16, 17

Equipped ...... II Timothy 3:17

Eternally secure ...... John 3:16

F

Forgiven …

If we confess our sins,
He is faithful and just to *forgive* us our sins,
and cleanse us from all unrighteousness.
1 John 1:9 KJV

*He is faithful to **forgive!***
And then He cleanses us from
__all__ unrighteousness!
Not just some of our sins.
ALL!
Oh that we would take Him at His word,
and believe in His divine forgiveness.
This is what frees us to become
all that God desires.

We tend to hold on to our sin
after we have repented of it.
We allow ourselves to be
shackled to our past sins,
which become the shame
that so often keeps us from God.

Much of the depression that has
taken hold in the Christian's life
is due to the lack of faith in
His forgiveness.
The past has no future.
Let it go, and move forward
*in **knowing** that you are forgiven!*

F

Because of Christ I am .....

Fearfully and wonderfully made ...... Psalms 139:14

Favored ...... Psalms 5:12

Fear God ...... Psalms 5:12

Filled to the fullness of God ...... Colossians 2:9, 10

Filled with the fruit of righteousness ...... Philippians 1:11

Filled with Joy ...... John 17:13

Filled with the knowledge of His will ...... Colossians 1:9

Filled with hope in Christ ...... Colossians 1:27

Filled with life through Christ ...... Colossians 3:4

Follower of Christ ...... John 12:26

Foreknown ...... Romans 8:29

Foreordained ...... I Peter 1:20

Formed in the womb by God ...... Jeremiah 1:5

Free ... Romans 8:2

Freed from sin ...... Romans 6:7, 22

Friend of God ...... John 15:14, 15

G

God's gift to Christ ...

Father, I will that **they** also,
whom thou hast given me,
be with me where I am;
that they may behold my glory,
which thou hast given me:
for thou lovest me before
the foundations of the world.
John 17:24 KJV

God's manifestation of love toward His Son was to
give Him us.
We are His treasure!
I love the way Jesus talks to His Father.
With the same breath, Jesus thanks His Father
for giving Him His glory and us.
*He tells His Father that He longs for **us, His gifts**,*
to be close to Him.
He wants an intimate relationship with us.
I fall in love with Him over, and over,
as the magnitude of this verse
pierces my heart and settles
*into my **knowing**.*

G

Because of Christ I am ...

Gifted ...... Romans 12:6

Given of all things ...... Romans 8:32

Given His magnificent promises ...... II Peter 1:3, 4

Given the Holy Spirit as a pledge ...... II Corinthians 1:22

Given rest ...... Matthew 12:28, 29

God's gift to Christ ...... John 17:24

Granted grace in Christ Jesus ...... Romans 5:17, 20

Guarded by God ...... II Timothy 1:12

Guarded by God's peace ...... Philippians 4:7

Guided ...... Psalm 48:14

H

His ...

But now thus saith the Lord that created thee, O Jacob,
and that formed thee, O Israel,
fear not; for I have redeemed thee,
I have called thee by thy name;
Thou art mine.
Isaiah 43:1 KJV

His.
No other word in all the scripture
captures my heart like this one word.
It is what I come home to
each time my heart begins to wander.
I whisper it in the hushed
moments of my days.
My heart rises high into my chest
*as it fills with the **knowing***
*that I am **His**.*

H

Because of Christ I am ...

the Handiwork of Christ ...... Ephesians 2:10

an Heir ...... Galatians 3:29 & Galatians 4:7

Helped by Him ...... Isaiah 44:2

Hidden with Christ in God ...... Colossians 3:12

Holy and dearly loved ...... Colossians 3:12

Holy and blameless ...... Ephesians 1:4

Holy ...... Hebrews 10:10

Honored ...... II Timothy 2:21

Hopeful ...... Romans 15:4, 13

His Love, His Dove ...... Song of Solomon 2:14

His Undefiled ...... I Peter 1:4 & James 1:27

I

Inscribed in the palms of His hands …

Behold, I have ***inscribed*** thee upon the palms of my hands;
Thy walls are continually before me.
Isaiah 49:16 KJV

As Christ knelt in the Garden,
it was my voice that He heard.
He listened to my cries of loss and pain.
He saw me in the street when I knelt over the lifeless body
of my two-year-old daughter.
He watched me sobbing in the night.
He heard my inner moaning when I begged Him to
"Just let me die!"
He knew me then and He knows me now.
I was on His mind as He carried the cross to Calvary.
*The scars in **His hands bear my name**.*
When I enter Heaven's gates, and I see Him face to face,
I will behold His splendor.
He will reach out His nail scarred hands to me.
I will cast my crown at His feet, and cry;
"Holy, holy, holy, Lord God, Almighty!"

I

Because of Christ I am ...

the Image and glory of God ...... I Corinthians 11:7

In Christ Jesus ...... I Corinthians 1:30

Indestructible ...... I Peter 1:23

Indwelt by Christ Jesus ...... John 14:20

Indwelt by His Spirit ...... Romans 8:35

Inseparable from His love ...... Romans 8:35

an Instrument of righteousness ...... Romans 6:13

Interceded for by the Spirit ...... Romans 8:26

Interceded for by Christ ...... Romans 8:34

J

Because of Christ I am …

a *Joint heir with Christ* …

The Spirit Himself bears witness with our spirit
that we are children of God, and if children, then heirs —
heirs of God and **joint heirs with Christ**,
if indeed we suffer with Him,
that we may also be glorified together.
Romans 8:16-17 NKJV

*When my grandmother Cora died at the age of 91,
a young relative asked his father what they would inherit from her.
It was a poignant question from the mind of an innocent child.
Grandma had 12 children, 58 grandchildren,
and 120 great-grandchildren.
She never held a job, she never drove a car.
But the pages of her bible were worn thin by
hands of love and devotion.*

*The boy's father responded with wisdom.
He told his son about the rich heritage left to us
by our grandmother.
There would be no money or wealth of this earth.
But she had left us the greatest gift.
She gave us Jesus.
She led her family to Christ.
From generation to generation this gift has been passed on.
Because of her faithfulness and un-ending prayers,
we have inherited the kingdom of God.
We are **heirs** and **joint heirs with Christ**.
No earthly treasure can compare.*

K

Kept …

Who are **kept** by the power of God
through faith unto salvation
ready to be revealed in the last time.
1 Peter 1:5 NIV

*My son Lyle loves to jump from
the third step of our staircase into my arms.
For the past few weeks he has been slowly making his way
up the stairs, wanting to jump from a higher level.
As his courage rises, so does his faith in me.
However, my ability to catch a 50 pound 3 year-old
has been challenged.
If he continues to climb higher,
I will have to tell him no.
There are limits to my strength and there is a risk
that he will get hurt.*

*God calls us to be as trusting, willing, and teachable
as we were in childhood.
He stands at the edge of our life
with His arms open wide,
and bids us; "Come, I will catch you."
Contrary to our human abilities,
there is no limit to God's strength.
He will always catch us.
We need only reach out and take hold
of the life He has prepared for us.
He **keeps** us!*

K

Because of Christ I am …

a **K**ing and a Priest ...... Revelation 1:6

Knowledgeable that all things work for good ...... Romans 8:

Knowledgeable in whom I believe ...... II Timothy 1:2

Known ...... II Timothy 2:19

L

Lavished with forgiveness ...

In Him we have redemption through His blood,
the forgiveness of sins,
in accordance with the riches of God's grace
that he **lavished** on us with all wisdom and understanding.
Ephesians 1:7,8 NKJV

I love what God has given to me in abundance.
He opened His arms and He died for me.
God, in all His wisdom,
understood my need for redemption.
From the abundant riches of God's grace,
*He **lavishes** me with forgiveness.*
He pours out His forgiveness freely,
to the point of overflowing.
I am rich.

L

Because of Christ I am ...

Lacking no wisdom ...... James 1:5

Led in Christ's triumph ...... II Corinthians 2:14

Laying aside the old self ...... Ephesians 4:22-24

filled with Life abundant ...... I John 4:9 & John 10:10

Light of the world ...... Matthew 5:14

Like a watered garden ...... Isaiah 58:11

Living for Him ...... II Corinthians 5:15

Living in Christ's life ...... Galatians 2:20

a Living stone ...... I Peter 2:5

the Lord's ...... Isaiah 44:5

Loved constantly and unconditionally ...... Isaiah 43:4

M

More than a conqueror …

Nay, in all these things we are ***more than conquerors***
through Him that loved us.
For I am persuaded, that neither death, nor life,
nor angels, nor principalities, nor powers,
nor things present, nor things to come.
nor height, nor depth, nor any other creature,
shall be able to separate us from the love of God,
which is in Christ Jesus our Lord.
Romans 8:37-39 KJV

There is nothing we can do to make God love us more.
There is nothing we can do to make God to love us less.
He loves us right now, right where we are.
Yet, the depth of His love will not let us settle for
less than all we can be.
I am so secure in the knowledge of God's love for me,
that when trouble approaches,
I conquer!
*I am **more than a conquer**, because Jesus branded His name*
across my heart when He died on the cross for me.
He rose from the dead and His Spirit dwells within me.
When I breathe, He breathes.
When I hurt, He hurts.
When I conquer, He conquers!
My heart beats, and He is home.

M

Because of Christ I am ...

Made alive with Christ ...... Ephesians 2:5

Made by Him ...... Psalms 100:3

a Member of His body ...... I Corinthians 12:27

a Minister of reconciliation ...... II Corinthians 5:18, 19

Mounted up with wings as eagles ...... Isaiah 40:31

N

Never alone ...

Let your conversation be without covetousness;
and be content with such things as ye have:
For He hath said,
I will ***never leave thee***, nor forsake thee.
Hebrews 13:5 KJV

I have sat in darkness.
I have lived in the pit.
I have been betrayed by a friend,
and hated by people I love.
I have been called crazy.
I have been abandoned by man.
I have been lonely.
But, I have never been alone!

God has always been here.
His voice is soft and kind.
It woos me. It enfolds me.
It embraces me with sweetness
that I no longer want to resist.
I am safe in the arms of my God.
Never alone.

N

Because of Christ I am ...

Near to God ...... Ephesians 2:13

Named ...... Isaiah 43:1

a New creation ...... II Corinthians 5:17

have a New life ...... Romans 6:4

New ...... Ephesians 4:22, 24

Not Condemned ...... Romans 8:1

No longer a child ...... Ephesians 4:14, 15

No longer a slave to sin ...... Romans 6:6

Not given a spirit of fear ...... II Timothy 1:7

Not my own ...... I Corinthians 6:19

Not weary ...... Isaiah 40:31

Noticed with loving concern ...... Psalm 33:13, 14

O

an Over-comer ...

For whatsoever is born of God,
overcometh the world: and this is the victory
that ***overcometh*** the world, even our faith.
Who is he that ***overcometh*** the world,
but he that believeth that
Jesus is the Son of God.
I John 5:4, 5 KJV

There are times in life when it feels like
I am walking through mud.
Not just a little mud around my feet,
but I am up to my hips in it.
At these times, I turn to this truth.
*I will **overcome** because*
I know that Jesus is the Son of God!
Everything else is very small next to this truth.
I know the last chapter of the book.
I know how it ends.
I win.
Because I am born of God!

O

Because of Christ I am ...

an **O**bject of mercy ...... Romans 9:23

Of God's household ...... Ephesians 2:19

On the winning side ...... Colossians 2:15

One with Him ...... John 17:23, 24

One Spirit with Him ...... I Corinthians 6:17

Obtaining an inheritance ...... Ephesians 1:10,11

P

Protected …

But the Lord is faithful,
and He will strengthen and ***protect you***
from the evil one.
11 Thessalonians 3:3 NIV

Sleep comes softly.
There is no fear when I am cradled
in the mighty arms of my heavenly Father.

P

Because of Christ I am ...

a **P**artaker of Christ ...... Hebrews 3:14

a **P**artaker of the divine nature of Christ ...... II Peter 1:4

a **P**artaker of grace ...... Philippians 1:7

a **P**artaker of the promise of Christ ...... Ephesians 3:6

Perfect and complete ...... James 1:2-4

a **P**ilgrim and stranger of the earth ...... Hebrews 11:13

a **P**ossessor of all things ...... I Corinthians 3:21

Prayed for ...... Luke 22:32

Predestined to adoption ...... Ephesians 1:5,11

Prepared beforehand for Glory ...... Romans 9:23

Presented to God holy and blameless ...... Colossians 1:22

Pressing forward ...... Philippians 3:14

Provided for ...... Matthew 6:33

Purchased ...... Revelation 5:9

Purpose driven ...... Psalm 138:8

Publisher of salvation ...... Isaiah 52:7

Q

Qualified …

Giving thanks unto the Father,
which hath **qualified** us to be partakers
of the inheritance of the saints in the light.
Who hath delivered us from the power of darkness,
and hath translated us into the kingdom of
His dear Son:
In whom we have redemption through the blood,
even the forgiveness of sin.
Colossians 1:12-14 KJV

I remember being in gym class as a child,
waiting in a line hoping that someone
would choose me for their team.
I was so miserable standing there.
The fear that I would be the last one chosen made me ill.
In most instances, my name was never even called.
I was a small freckled little thing with wild curly hair.

Even now, I can feel that ache
in the pit of my stomach as I recall the grumbling voices
of the team that got stuck with me.
In the eyes of so many, I was not qualified.

I praise God that He has qualified me
by the shedding of Christ's blood.
I am not standing in line waiting.
He calls my name.
I am walking in the light of my true inheritance.
I am a child of the King.
Qualified

R

Refined ...

Wherein ye greatly rejoice,
though now for a season, if need be,
ye are in heaviness through manifold temptations:
That the trial of your faith, being much more precious
than of gold that perisheth, though it **be tried with fire**,
might be found unto praise and honor and glory at
the appearing of Jesus Christ.
I Peter 1:6, 7 KJV

Rejoice in my trials?!
Here is a wonderful treasure from scripture.
Oh, that we would take hold of this powerful truth.
To know that in the midst of our most life-shattering trials,
*we are being **made beautiful**.*
To be fully aware of this truth at the very height of our pain
brings unspeakable joy.
So often we miss the blessings of this promise because
we focus on the pain instead of the promise.
Purpose in your heart and mind that the next time
troubles come, you will rejoice!
*God is **refining you**.*
And you will be beautiful at Christ's appearing!

R

Because of Christ I am ...

Ransomed ...... Matthew 20:28

able to Receive Mercy ...... I Peter 2:10

able to Receive the unshakable kingdom ...... Hebrews 12:28

able to Receive the riches of grace ...... Ephesians 1:7

Reconciled to God ...... Romans 5:10

Redeemed ...... Galatians 3:13

Raised up with Christ ...... Ephesians 2:6, 7

Reigning in life ...... Romans 5:17

Rejoicing ...... Romans 5:2,3

Renewed ...... II Corinthians 4:16

a Representative of God ...... Matthew 5:16

given Rest ...... Matthew 11:28-30

Rewarded by God ...... Isaiah 49:4

Rich ...... II Corinthians 8:9

Righteous ...... Romans 3:22,26

Rooted and built up ...... Colossians 2:7

Royalty ...... Romans 5:17, 8: 16, 17

S

Safe ...

I will both lay me down in peace, and sleep;
For thou, Lord, only
makest me dwell in **safety**.
Psalm 4:8 KJV

Saved through faith ...

But God, who is rich in mercy,
for His great love wherewith He loved us,
even when we were dead in sins,
hath quickened us together with Christ.
For by grace are ye **saved through faith**;
and that not of yourselves:
it is the gift of God.
Ephesians 2:4,5,8 KJV

Set free ...

Then you shall know the truth,
And the truth will **set you free**.
John 8:32 KJV

*God said you will **know** the truth, and the truth will **set you free**.
He did not say you will "hear" the truth,
and the truth will set you free.
We must get the truth into the deepest part of our **knowing**.
You may have heard about God, but do you know Him*

S

Because of Christ I am ...

a Saint ...... Romans 1:7

the Salt of the earth ...... Matthew 5:13

Sanctified ...... I Thessalonians 5:23

Satisfied ...... Psalm 17:15

Seated in heavenly places ...... Ephesians 2:6

Secure ...... Deuteronomy 33:12

Sent ...... John 20:21

a Servant ...... Romans 6:22

a Slave of righteousness ...... Romans 6:18

a Soldier ...... II Timothy 2:3,4

a Sower and Reaper ...... John 4:37

Sprinkled with clean water ...... Ezekiel 36:25

Stable ...... Isaiah 33:6

Standing ...... Romans 5:2

Standing firm in Christ ...... II Corinthians 1:21

Strengthened by Him ...... Ephesians 3:16

Strong in the Lord ...... Ephesians 6:10

Sustained from birth ...... Psalm 71:6

the Sweet aroma of God ...... II Corinthians 2:14,15

T

Thought about …

How precious also are thy thoughts unto me, *O God!*
How great is the sum of them!
If I should count them, they are more in number than the sand:
When I awake, I am still with thee.
Psalm 139:17, 18 KJV

God thinks about me.
A lot.

T

Because of Christ I am ...

the Temple of the living God ...... II Corinthians 3:16 & 6:19

Thought about ...... Psalm 139:17, 18

Transformed to the kingdom of His Son ...... Colossians 1:13

Transformed into His image ...... II Corinthians 3:18

Treasured possession ...... John 17:7

In Truth ...... John 17:7

U

Undefiled …

I sleep, but my heart waketh;
it is the voice of my beloved that knocketh, saying,
"Open to me my sister, my love, my dove,
my *undefiled…*"
Song of Solomon 5:2 KJV

One awful, wonderful night, as I travailed before God,
He came to me and whispered this verse
from Song of Solomon into my heart.
I have done some wicked things with my life.
I have done things that I will never be able to talk about.
There were ugly, despicable acts of self-indulgence.
I should have gone to prison for some of the things I did.
But here I am, saved by God's amazing grace.
God looks at me and sees the blood of His Son poured out for my
sins.
He whispers to me:
*"You are my **undefiled**."*
I surrender to Him: "Yes Lord, I am."

54

U

Because of Christ I am …

Unafraid …… Isaiah 44:2, 51:12

Understood …… Ephesians 1:8

Understanding things given by God …… II Corinthians 2:12

United with Christ …… Romans 6:5

Unworthy …… I Corinthians 4:7

Useful for his glory …… Isaiah 4:3,7

Upheld …… Isaiah 41:10

V

Because of Christ I am ...

Valued ...

Look at the birds of the air;
they do not sow or reap, or store away in barns,
and yet your heavenly Father feeds them.
Are you not much more ***valuable*** than they?
Matthew 6:26 NIV

A wise man told me that
the value of an item is determined by
what someone is willing to pay for it.
God paid for me with His life.
*I am **valued** above all things.*

Victorious ...... I Corinthians 15:57

W

Waiting for our Savior ...

Looking for that blessed hope,
and the glorious appearing
of the great God and
our Savior Jesus Christ.
Titus 2:13

*I am **waiting** and watching, and looking for Him.*
I search the skies for Him.
My heart aches with a longing, I can not explain.
I whisper to Him;
"Master, Savior, my Adonai ...
Jesus, you are my everything."

W

Because of Christ I am ...

Walking in new life ...... Romans 6:4

Washed ...... Titus 2:13

Wise ...... James 1:5

a Witness of Christ ...... Acts 1:8

a Wonder ...... Psalm 71:7

a Worshipper of Christ ...... Psalm 95:6

X

Because of Christ I am …

*given **Charis** …*

The Greek letter "X," which resembles our English letter "X," is translated as "ch."

Charis, pronounced *Khar'-ece,* is the Greek word meaning *grace.*

And of His fullness have all we received, and **grace** for **grace.**
For the law was given by Moses but **grace** and truth came by Jesus Christ.
John 1:16, 17 KJV

By whom we have received **grace** and the apostleship,
for obedience to the faith among all nations,
for His name sake.
Romans 1:5 KJV

For all have sinned, and fallen short of the glory of God;
being justified freely,
by His **grace** through the redemption that is in
Christ Jesus.
Romans 3:23, 24 KJV

Now our Lord Jesus Christ Himself, and God, even our Father,
which hath loved us, and hath given us
everlasting consolation and good hope through **grace**,
comfort your hearts, and stablish you in every good word and
work.
II Thessalonians 2:16, 17

***Charis** also means Joy*

Y

Yielded to God ...

But ***yield*** yourselves to God
as men who have been brought
from death to life,
and your members to God
as instruments of righteousness.
Romans 6:13 NIV

I am His.
I was God's idea from the very beginning.
He gave me life.
All that I am, and all that I have,
was given to me by God.
These truths put "self" to death.
I belong to the God who created all things.
This awesome God became a servant, and walked among us,
and then He died to rescue me.
I no longer struggle or try to pull away.
*I can **yield** to all that He requires, because*
*I **know** that He loves me.*

Z

Because of Christ I am …

Zealous …

Who gave Himself for us,
that He might redeem us from all iniquity,
and purify unto Himself
a peculiar people,
zealous of good works.
Titus 2: 14 KJV

Zealous: *Fanatical, Passionate, Obsessive
Eager, Enthusiastic, Fervent, Fixated*

Peculiar: *Odd, Strange, Irregular, Unusual
Atypical, Remarkable, Extraordinary, Uncommon*

*Do any of these words describe you?
Are you zealous for God?
He gave His life to purify us into becoming peculiar,
zealous people for Himself.
He desires our passion even at the risk of looking fanatical.
If we are His redeemed, we are different
from those who do not know Him.*

*We are to be like Christ.
People rejected and hated Him.
There was nothing about Him that would attract us to Him.
He is God.
Yet He lowered Himself to become our servant.
His friends and family accused Him of being a lunatic;
they said He was out of His mind.
They could not fathom **this kind of love**.*

Journal

Use these next pages to record your daily travels on your journey to
A Place Called Knowing.
As God begins to reveal Himself to you, take the time to
map out the path He leads you on. Trace the joy and the pain of
Discovering Your Identity In Christ.

We are all the work of thy hand. Isaiah 64:8

Let us consider on another to provoke unto love and to good works.
Hebrews 10:24

Lead me in thy truth, and teach me. Psalm 25:5

With the Lord there is mercy, and with Him is
plenteous redemption. Psalm 130:7

Follow me and I will make you fishers of men. Matthew 4:19

Happy is that people ... whose God is the Lord. Psalm 144:15

The Lord shall preserve thee from all evil; He shall preserve thy soul.
Psalm 121:7

Not my will, but thine, be done. Luke 22:42

Except a man be born again, he cannot see the kingdom of God.
John 3:3

Let us consider one another to provoke unto love and to
good works. Hebrews 10:24

Rejoice in the Lord always; and again I say rejoice. Philippians 4:4

_____
_____
_____
_____
_____
_____
_____
_____
_____
_____
_____
_____
_____
_____
_____
_____
_____
_____
_____
_____
_____
_____
_____
_____
_____
_____
_____
_____
_____
_____
_____
_____
_____
_____
_____
_____

His name shall be called Wonderful ... The Mighty God ...
Prince of Peace... Isaiah 9:6

There is one God, one mediator between God and men ...
Jesus Christ. I Timothy 2:5

_____
_____
_____
_____
_____
_____
_____
_____
_____
_____
_____
_____
_____
_____
_____
_____
_____
_____
_____
_____
_____
_____
_____
_____
_____
_____
_____
_____
_____
_____
_____
_____
_____
_____
_____
_____

… Fear the Lord, and serve Him in sincerity and in truth.
Joshua 24:14

Let him ask in faith, nothing wavering. James 1:6

The Lord is my light and my salvation. Psalm 27:1

_____

_____

_____

_____

_____

_____

_____

_____

_____

_____

_____

_____

_____

_____

_____

_____

_____

_____

_____

_____

_____

_____

_____

_____

_____

_____

_____

_____

_____

_____

God so loved the world, that He gave His only begotten son …
John 3:16

… Love one another with a pure heart fervently. I Peter 1:22

Blessed are they that have not seen, and yet have believed.
John 20:29

The effectual fervent prayer of a righteous man availeth much.
James 5:16

There is a friend that sticketh closer than a brother. Proverbs 18:24

He took them up in His arms, put His hands upon them,
and blessed them. Mark 10:16

"He that hath seen me, hath seen the Father." John 14:9

We are the clay, and thou art the potter. Isaiah 64:8

We love Him, because He firsts loved us. I John 4:19

Then will I sprinkle clean water upon you, and you shall be clean …
Ezekiel 36:25

A new heart also will I give you, and a new spirit will I put
within you… Ezekiel 36:26a

...and I will take away the stony heart out of your flesh...
Ezekiel 36:26b

… and I will give you an heart of flesh. Ezekiel 36:26b

_____
_____
_____
_____
_____
_____
_____
_____
_____
_____
_____
_____
_____
_____
_____
_____
_____
_____
_____
_____
_____
_____
_____
_____
_____
_____
_____
_____
_____
_____
_____
_____
_____
_____
_____
_____

And I will put my spirit within you, and cause you to walk in
my statutes. Ezekiel 36:27a

Now is the day of salvation. I Corinthians 6:2

Thy God hath commanded thy strength. Psalm 68:28

He healed the broken hearted ... Psalm 147:3

_____
_____
_____
_____
_____
_____
_____
_____
_____
_____
_____
_____
_____
_____
_____
_____
_____
_____
_____
_____
_____
_____
_____
_____
_____
_____
_____
_____
_____
_____
_____
_____
_____

Lift your eyes to hills from where cometh thy strength …
Psalms 121:1

To be spiritually minded is life and peace. Romans 8:6

For me to live is Christ ... Philippians 1:21

In all thy ways acknowledge Him, and He shall direct thy paths.
Proverbs 3:6

Take fast hold of instruction ... for she is thy life. Proverbs 4:13

But He was wounded for our transgressions, He was bruised
for our iniquities… Isa 53:5

Lo, these are parts of His ways, but how little a portion
is heard of Him? Job 2614a

...but the thunder of His *shtenoo* (power) who can understand?
Job 26:14b

If the son of man shall make you free, ye shall be free indeed.
John 8:36

And whosoever will be chief among you, let him be your servant.
Matthew 20:27

"You have not chosen me, but I have chosen you ..."
John 15:16a

Before I formed thee in the womb, I knew thee … Jeremiah 1:5

... Let every man be swift to hear, slow to speak, slow to wrath.
James 1:19

For I know the plans I have for you....thoughts of peace ...
Jeremiah 29:11

When my father and mother forsake me, the Lord will take me up …
Psalm 27:10

Thou wilt keep him in perfect peace, whose mind is stayed on thee ...
Isaiah 26:3

Create in me a clean heart. O God; and renew a right spirit within me.
Psalm 51:10

I can do all things through Christ who gives me strength ...
Philippians 4:13

My soul clings to you; your right hand upholds me. Psalm 63:8

Printed in the United States
30972LVS00005B/181-228